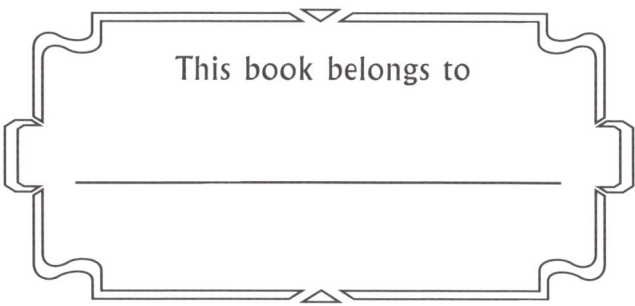

CHARACTERS
Buffalo Biff - Asa Wiggins
Ruby - Katie Stewart
Johnny - Joseph-Aaron Tanifum
Rosa Parks - Maria Covington
Martin Luther King, Jr. - Victor Hannah
Bus Driver - Robert White Johnson
Officer - Chris Fenton

Recorded by: Open Door Productions
Talent Directed by: Brian T. Cox/Don Jarvis
Executive Producer: Cheryl J. Hutchinson
Developed and Created by: Toy Box Productions
Story Written by: James Collins
Art Direction and Character Illustrations by:
Brian T. Cox for Toy Box Productions

Manufactured exclusively by
CRT, Custom Products, Inc.
℗ © 2005 Toy Box Productions,
A Division of CRT, Custom Products, Inc.
7532 Hickory Hills Court,
Whites Creek, TN 37189

1-800-750-1511   www.crttoybox.com

ISBN: 1-932332-17-0

Welcome to another
Time Traveler's Adventure.

We're headed back to the 1950's to learn about Rosa Parks and how she became known as the Mother of the Civil Rights Movement.

Hold on as we blast through time with
Buffalo Biff and Farley's Raiders!

Changing The World

Johnny: Hey, those stories our teacher told us were fascinating, weren't they?

Biff: Yeah, they were cool. Sorry you missed it Ruby. Are the rehearsals for the school play going well?

Ruby: It's great fun, but hard work, too. I had to get involved, especially after my mom said art can change the world.

Johnny: Well, computers sure changed things. My dad said when he was a kid, the only way to get information was to read encyclopedias.

Ruby: Encyclo what?

Biff: Very funny, Ruby. Today many people use the internet to get information.

turn page

Johnny: Well, my family talked about changing the world last night. We have relatives visiting from out of town. My grandfather's brother was involved in some early civil rights work.

Biff: So, there are lots of ways to change the world; art, computers and standing up for something you believe in.

Johnny: Or maybe sitting down. Ruby, have you heard of Rosa Parks?

Ruby: Is she a famous actress or singer?

Johnny: No, she was just a regular person.

Biff: But she was someone who helped change the world. Hey, tomorrow is Saturday. Let's meet at the lab early and get the time machine ready and see some history!

Ruby: Wait a minute. Now, I recall her famous bus ride in Alabama and from what I read, the segregated south was kind of dangerous. How scary is this?

Johnny: Changing the world is always scary.

turn page

Johnny: After burners are clear, Biff.

Ruby: Everything's tightened up on this side.

Biff: Check. Now, make sure both of you have some of these coins. They were all minted before 1955. And let's see, we all have period clothes, so that's check and check.

Ruby: Are you sure actually being there on the bus is a good idea?

Biff: It's dangerous, but it makes sense. We'll just be there in the crowd, observing. Is that clear? We can not interact. Ok?

Johnny: We definitely don't want to alter anything in this situation.

Biff: All right, climb in and buckle up. Ruby, check the Biffometer while I get Farley. In you go, Farley.

Farley: Ruff, Ruff.

Ruby: Yes, it's still set for December 1, 1955. Montgomery, Alabama.

Biff: Ok. I'm ready. Here we go!

All: Yahoo!

turn page

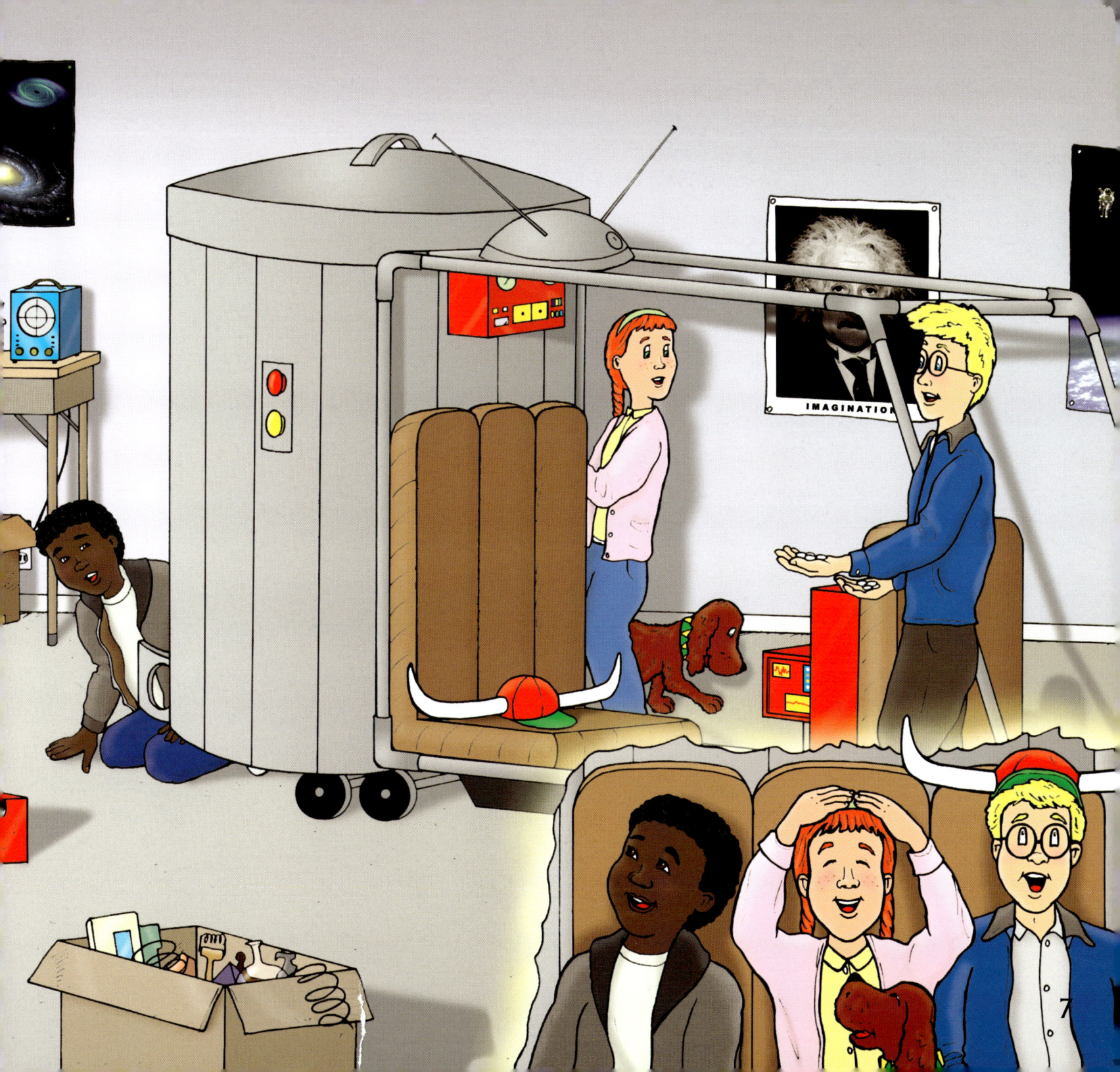

That's Segregation

Johnny: You know, Biff, being there on the bus will complicate things. We'll be separated.

Ruby: What do you mean? Why can't you sit with us?

Biff: That's segregation. The law had the bus seating divided. White people sat up front and African-Americans had to sit in the rear.

Ruby: You're kidding me, right? How could this happen in America, the land of the free?

Johnny: Well, America's history isn't always pretty. It took almost a hundred years for blacks to get from slaves to the status of being second class citizens.

Ruby: How could something like using a person's color as a reason for anything last so long? It sounds simply stupid and silly.

Biff: Well, that's the beauty of non-violence. By exposing the stupidity of some issue, people can see how unfair it is and then change it.

turn page

Ruby: This is beginning to sound like there was a lot to change and sounds more silly than scary.

Biff: Life in the fifties was a little crazy.

Johnny: And the world had to change. It was the right time to change what was so wrong.

Biff: Ok. Here we are. Look for the department store.

Ruby: You have a sudden urge to go shopping?

Biff: Very funny. Rosa Parks worked as a seamstress in the department store.

Johnny: We're shopping for history, remember? There it is. Let's go around and find a place to park the time machine.

turn page

Too Many Doors

Ruby: Look! That door is marked as the white entrance. Why would they do that? Is there a blue or orange one?

Johnny: No, Ruby. That's another sign of segregation. It's the color code. Only white people can enter through that door.

Biff: Watch as we circle the building. Ok, here's the colored entrance. This is where African-Americans had to enter the store.

Ruby: Oh, I get it. This segregation thing is not only stupid, it's rude.

Johnny: You've got that right, Ruby. Hey Biff, that alley looks like a good place.

Biff: Right you are. We'll park here. Farley, you guard the time machine, o.k. boy?

Farley: Ruff, ruff.

turn page

Ruby: Now let's not get lost. Make sure we can find this place again.

Biff: Everyone have their coins so we can get on the bus?

Ruby: Yes, I've got mine.

Johnny: Me, too. I'm ready.

Biff: Ok, the time machine is secure and it's about time for Rosa Parks to get off work.

Johnny: Then let's go and see history up close and personal.

turn page

Rosa Gets Onboard

Biff: Remember, we just observe. Don't talk with anyone.

Johnny: Let's look on the lighter side here. When we get on the bus, we'll see history from both directions, from the back and from the front.

Ruby: Well, I'm glad you can keep a sense of humor about this. I'm feeling scared again.

turn page

Ruby: Is that her? She looks too tired to change the world. This bus isn't very crowded.

Biff: Not yet. But just wait. Look, she sits just behind the white section.

Johnny: Ok, I'll sit near the back. I'll see you afterwards and we'll compare notes.

turn page

Bus Driver: The bus is loading up, so just pay your fare and go around to your entrance.

Ruby: You mean to tell me black people have to pay their fare, get off the bus and walk around to the rear door to re-enter?

Biff: Yes, and sometimes they didn't even make it in time. Shhh.

Bus Driver: Hey you folks, move to the rear of the bus.

Ruby: But all the seats are filled back there. He's so mean. I'm glad Rosa Parks stayed in her seat.

Biff: Yeah, but now the driver has stopped the bus. He sees the white section is full.

turn page

Bus Driver: You heard me lady. Move to the rear of the bus. Hey! Are you deaf? I told you to move to the rear and give up your seat so a white person can sit down!

Rosa Parks: No! I will not!

Bus Driver: What? I can have you arrested, you know!

Rosa Parks: Well, I guess you could do that!

turn page

Bus Driver: Officer! Officer! Come over here will you! I've got this troublemaker who won't move to the rear and give up her seat!

Officer: Ma'am, why don't you give up your seat and move to the rear?

Rosa Parks: I don't think I should have to. I paid my fare! I was seated first! Why are you pushing me around?

Officer: Ma'am, the law is the law and it says I have to place you under arrest if you don't give up your seat.

Rosa Parks: I'm not some second class citizen! I don't appreciate being treated this unfairly!

turn page

25

Johnny: They're putting handcuffs on her and putting her into a police car.

Ruby: Wow! I can't believe this. I've never seen someone get arrested.

Biff: Ok, that's our cue. Let's get off here before he starts the bus again. Come on, Johnny.

turn page

Biff: This man is calling the NAACP office to tell them what has just happened. That the police just arrested a quiet black woman for not giving up her seat. Let's get back to the time machine.

Ruby: What is the NAACP?

Biff: The letters mean National Association of the Advancement of Colored People.

Johnny: They're a group that works for racial equality. It's the one my grandfather's brother helped when he was a young man. He said it was tough in the early days. Seeing how mean that driver was, I believe him. I didn't know what was going to happen.

Ruby: I was more scared than she was. Rosa Parks didn't look scared. She looked more annoyed.

turn page

Johnny: Hi Farley. How would you feel if you were made to give up your seat?

Farley: Grrrrrr.

Biff: Let's follow them. Buckle up and off we go.

turn page

Challenging The Laws

Ruby: Well, I don't see the world changing yet.

Johnny: This is only the beginning of our adventure. You'll see.

Biff: Here they come.

Ruby: Who's they? What's happening?

Biff: Mr. Parks, Rosa's husband, has been joined by a representative of the NAACP to post bail. A Mr. E.D. Nixon, I believe.

Ruby: Oh I see. They are here to help her.

Biff: Of course, but the NAACP has been looking for someone respectable, employed and married so they can begin to challenge the segregation laws.

Johnny: The whole black community is tired of being treated so unfairly by these laws. Rosa wants to be the last person to be mistreated so she decides to help them.

Biff: This is Thursday. Let's move ahead and see what happens tomorrow.

turn page

MLK: Good people, I know I have only recently moved to this fine community of Montgomery as your minister but we must join with Rosa Parks. Once again, we are faced with the struggle to gain equality. Now Mr. Nixon has asked me to call for and lead this boycott of the city bus system. Please join us.

Biff: This is where it starts to get interesting. You see, the bus system relies heavily on the African-American community.

Johnny: And if they stop riding the buses, the city will start losing money.

Ruby: Oh, and all those flyers are to be spread around the community to enlist support.

Biff: Yes, and they have to work fast because they want to start the boycott on Monday.

Ruby: How will an entire community get to and from work or to stores?

Johnny: Some will walk, others will carpool. They'll even ride bikes and of course the NAACP will help provide some alternate transportation.

Ruby: Wow, this is quite an effort.

Biff: A real community effort. Let's move ahead to Monday.

turn page

35

A Good Start

Johnny: Look, the boycott leaders are watching to see whether or not their plan to start a boycott of the buses is going to work.

Ruby: It's off to a good start. So far, every bus that's passed us has been nearly empty with no African-Americans onboard.

Biff: Lets go across town and see what happens to Rosa Parks in court.

turn page

PLAZA FURNITU

37

Ruby: Is there any hope for justice here?

Biff: No, not really. Everyone is still following those uh, stupid laws that are in place.

Johnny: She's found guilty and the judge fines her fourteen dollars.

Biff: Mr. E.D. Nixon, the NAACP lawyer, pays her fine and declares the law unjust and says he'll appeal this ruling all the way to the Supreme Court.

Ruby: Gosh, that will take some time, won't it?

turn page

GUILTY! $14

39

MLK Speaks Out

MLK: I want to thank you all for joining us for the first day of our boycott. But we will have to prevail if we are to succeed. This is the time for us to say to those who have mistreated us for so long that we are tired of being segregated and humiliated. We must do this with no malice in our hearts. We must do this without violence. We must not react to anything they do to us.

Ruby: Well, it worked for a day but how long can all these people resist that easy bus ride to work.

Johnny: As long as it takes. You see, you have to be determined to change the world. It's never easy.

turn page

41

Biff: The next day the leaders of the boycott took three simple demands to the city commissioners and the bus company.

Ruby: Well, I can tell you right now, one of those demands was for the drivers to be nice to all their passengers.

Johnny: Yes, that's right. And another was that African-American passengers would stop having to give up their seats to white passengers.

Biff: And the last demand was for the bus company to start hiring African-American drivers.

Ruby: All their requests sound reasonable to me. So, is that the end to the story?

Biff: Not hardly. Both the city and the bus company said no.

Johnny: And that refusal only made the people protesting more determined and that's when the boycott leaders demanded an end to the bus segregation completely.

Biff: So let's go forward in time again. This time a few months ahead.

turn page

43

The Boycott Continues

Ruby: Oh, I see. So the bus boycott continued.

Biff: By now, the bus lines begin losing money because seventy-five percent of the riders were African-American and they all joined the boycott. Pretty soon the bus company had to cut back on the number of buses running. They also had to raise the price of a fare.

Johnny: Yeah, the bus company thought these poor working families would start using the buses again real soon. They sure were wrong.

Ruby: I bet not only the white bus riders were mad because they had to pay more, but also the shopkeepers were probably getting angry for losing business.

Johnny: Yes, but the black community stayed united and determined in the face of greater and greater levels of frustration. There were some acts of violence against them.

turn page

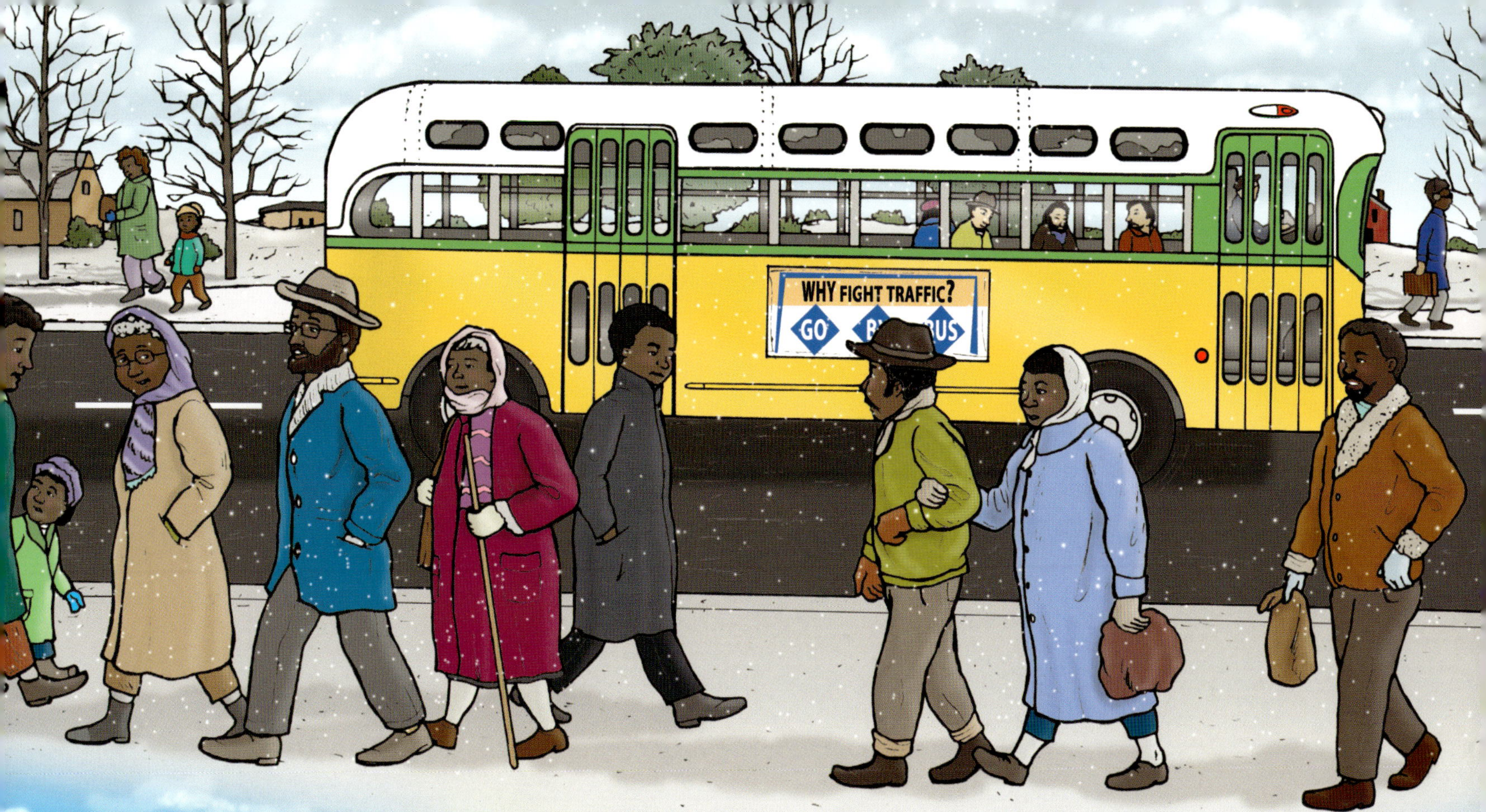
WHY FIGHT TRAFFIC?
GO
BUS

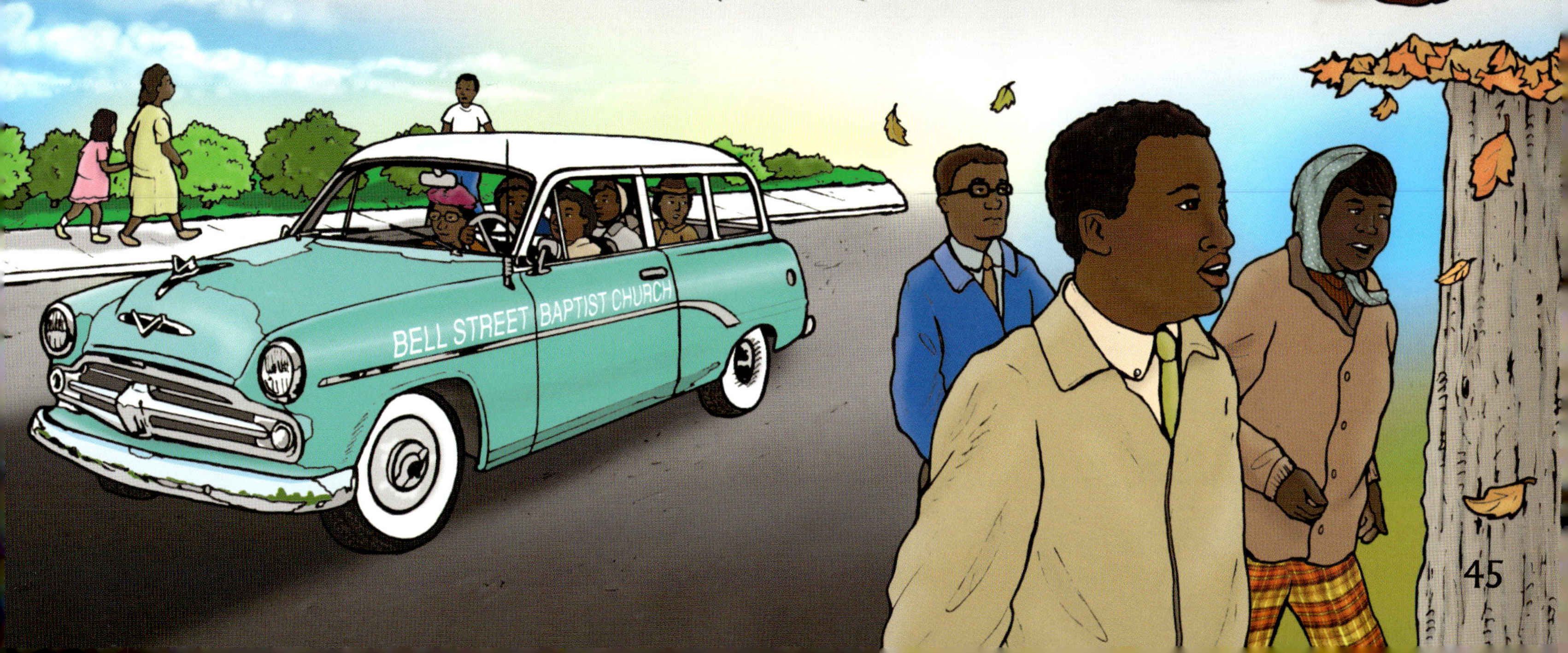
BELL STREET BAPTIST CHURCH

Biff: Through the whole thing, Reverand Martin Luther King used Rosa Parks as an example. He guided the boycotters to resist reacting with violence and to stay calm and use non-violence methods.

Ruby: It's always hard not to push back when someone pushes you.

Johnny: Yes, it is. It was hard for all the people. Some of the protest leaders received threatening phone calls.

Biff: Back then, they couldn't trace calls as easily as they can in our time. Homes were vandalized and even....

turn page

47

Ruby: Good heavens, what was that?

Johnny: Reverand King's house was bombed one night while he was at a church meeting.

Biff: But neither his wife or child were hurt.

Ruby: I'm glad no one was hurt.

Biff: When he was told, he rushed home. A lot of his supporters had had enough and crowded around his house like an angry mob. They were ready to fight back.

Johnny: But still, Reverend King urged the people to stay calm and continue their non-violent protest.

Ruby: It truly amazes me that so many people stayed so calm and protested so long after Rosa Parks said no.

Biff: Not only that, but Rosa Parks got fired from her job. But nothing could stop her from staying with the protest. The African-Americans stayed united and became even more determined.

turn page

49

Johnny: Let's jump forward to see the results of what Rosa Parks started.

Biff: I'm setting the Biffometer now.

Ruby: Wow! You mean it took nearly a year! This reads November 13, 1956!

Biff: Yes. That's when the case of Rosa Parks is ruled on by the Supreme Court.

Johnny: That was the day when the segregation laws in Montgomery were declared unconstitutional. A truly great day for America.

Ruby: So it was no longer legal to segregate people and be mean to them just because of their color.

Biff: Yes, and all I can say is, it was about time.

Johnny: No one will ever forget the name of Rosa Parks. She started this change in history.

Ruby: I never knew one person could create so much positive change.

turn page

51

Johnny: On the day after the Supreme Court ruling, Rosa Parks, Mr. E.D. Nixon and Reverend Martin Luther King boarded a Montgomery bus. Rosa Parks sat in the front for the first time in her life.

Ruby: Now I can see how life was changed for the better, for all Americans. Incredible!

Biff: Well, that's how Rosa Parks became the mother of the Civil Rights Movement.

Ruby: It was awesome to watch this history-making moment.

Biff: It's almost like putting a puzzle together. All the right pieces have to be there and fit. History is amazing!

Johnny: Yeah, just think. What would have happened if some of the original pieces weren't there? What if Reverend Martin Luther King wasn't the leader or Mr. E.D. Nixon was on vacation. Or even if that unknown man did not notify the NAACP right away. Wow!

turn page

53

Biff: Like you said earlier, Johnny, it was the right time for the right people to change what was so wrong for so long.

Ruby: Well, I'd like to know more about her. What else do you know, Johnny?

Johnny: Well, Rosa Parks was born on February 4th, 1913. She joined the NAACP in 1943 and was the secretary of the Montgomery chapter for a while. But the loss of her job at the department store caused her to move to Detroit, Michigan in 1957. Then in 1965, she worked on the staff of a US Representative until she retired in 1988.

Biff: I have to admit that up close view of history makes it personal. What do you say we head back home?

All: We're Buffalo Biff and Farley's Raiders! Yahoo!

Farley: Ruff, Ruff!

turn page

55

There's much more to learn about Rosa Parks
on the internet or at your local library.

Now it's your chance to become the character of your
choice in this Time Traveler's Adventure.

Get ready and have fun becoming one of
Farley's Raiders!